Simon Perril is a poet and collagist. His poetry publications include *In the Final Year of my 40s* (Shearsman, 2018), *Beneath* (Shearsman, 2015), *Archilochus on the Moon* (Shearsman, 2013), *Newton's Splinter* (Open House, 2012), *Nitrate* (Salt, 2010), *A Clutch of Odes* (Oystercatcher, 2009), and *Hearing is Itself Suddenly a Kind of Singing* (Salt, 2004). As a critic he has written widely on contemporary poetry, editing *The Salt Companion to John James*, and *Tending the Vortex: The Works of Brian Catling*. He is Professor of Poetic Practice at De Montfort University, in Leicester.

Also by Simon Perril

.

An asterisk denotes a Shearsman title.

Simon Perril

THE SLIP

Shearsman Books

First published in the United Kingdom in 2020 by
Shearsman Books Ltd
PO Box 4239
Swindon
SN3 9FN

Shearsman Books Ltd Registered Office
30–31 St. James Place, Mangotsfield, Bristol BS16 9JB
(this address not for correspondence)

www.shearsman.com

ISBN 978-1-84861-721-6

THE SLIP

at the end of a long journey
this one's for Elly,
and Gatehouse dreams

1.

night breathes caulk
exhales

I remember the ripple
of sails

their snap
as the wind broke

behind us
the ass's back

of Paros
– or was it Thasos?

Where poke
the bones of home?

2.

Hermes, sheep-thief be praised;
he says look upon the day
as a scabbed knee
to be picked upon

some scaly fruit
the body blooms
in friction 'gainst
this world's serrated edge.

Zeus' blade
is laid across the firmament;
and he slices
at our permanence

so we bake
served
in the dog days

3.

hail the potter
who lays liquid trays
under midday glare
that they may adopt weight

who finds there
the rudiments of shape
woven from water
and silt cake.

May we, similarly,
hear with our hands
the sound of the shape
held in clay
as we wedge at the edges of form

and throw it
into the felting dark

4.

I walk the standing water
that pools in the agora

it wets my ankles
gathers as I leak

I feel it lap
in the civic cracks

of morning mouths.
These inopportune fountains

spout

5.

being once a man
I can speak of it
as water runs away
from source.

I'll pause
in the speaking
for the course
is 'cross inhospitable ground;

and the sounds I'll make
shall take us some distance
in understanding
the persistent labour
of breathing

6.

I sit in the said
being force-fed Thasian pickle

by he who kept counsel
in Hera's precinct

with Dame Harangue
confected a sour paste

such thick marinate
of Parian iambs

served me stone, sent me
and my family

to beds
of cool marble

7.

The oracle plotted us
a path in riddle
replete with animal guide

'take,' shook the Pythia, 'a beast
in your midst; one might
use its stealth.'

There are a wealth of tracks
can't be landed
with the ingenuity of traps;

there are some acts,
slow to unfurl,
that outlive their maps

8.

dead people's things
few know
how keenly they sing

yet I'll hear them
at the ends
of both my daughters

notes left
in surrounding air.
My thought

turns to bedsheets
hung corner
to corner

9.

Telesicles, of all knots
Omphalos
binds us tight.
You recall, old friend,
the air drum-tight
at the world's navel

our descent
towards the grey
sea-spray of olives
at Amphissa;

how we were walled
by the Shining Cliffs
my knees
hobbled like a crane's.

Let us take, you said,
the weight off our feet
by the Castalian spring
regain your wolf-steps.

We did so,
and pressed on,
met the Kourai
at Delphi.

Friend, you bought me
a gift there, outside
the temple of Apollo;

a fine jug
of black-traced glaze

on one side Dolon
the trick-wolf tricked
on the other
Theseus joined freed slaves
a-twist in geranos.

Old friend, may I turn this yarn
back into its ball;
recall we sailed
at Delphic request
a bristling ship and supped
elsewhere.

We supped elsewhere.

10.

In the dappled dusk
outskirting the city,
I trudge the dustlands,

thirst my guide, Sirius
whose scorching bite
blights tree-bark

strikes swift, sharp
as the iridescent scabbard
of a snake;

stirs black bile
that slaps the sides
of my kettle-belly

a-brim
with an inner barking.
I cannot slake this want;

It is as if I have drooled
this silvered crucible
before me

pool of my riddling shape,
in which I make out
a liquid fox

its wet grin, red eyes
with the slanted pupils
of a cat

11.

a father overlooks.
This is his perennial task
and he asks

of the passage of light
its business; for if
it marks what it touches

his task
is to mask this. He has
no jurisdiction over the length of days

or their consumption
by shadow.
Still he overlooks,

would angle his branches
just so.
You know

there are compositions of shield
you'll not find
on any battlefield

12.

have you ever watched
a wavering clutch
of cypress

and concluded
we are aquatic;
and all around

and in us
is water,
its coiling passage.

And regret
is the seeking of exits
the seeping

of fig viscera
through the applied pressure
of a hungry mouth

13.

seek comfort, daughters,
for Mount Parnassus
wears a snow cap in spring.

Thus should we
be unafraid
to carry our colder portions;

aches and agues
are but distortions,
mere vapours, humours;

they take us
out of doors
out of sorts.

I applaud such a journey:
only in leaving
do we build a home

and send back reports
of what touch does,
and cartographers do not know

scraping outlines
climes and conquests.
Seek comfort, daughters

for never again will you fear
the scrape of oars
towards foreign shores

the transport of men
across watery skin
to alien quarters

14.

the crane knows,
feels tremors
in its hollow bones.

The unsettled earth
is in bad humour
spits and splits

and it's no wonder
there is blood
on the morrow;

we crossed seas
to greet it
carrying secrets in our spears

like frozen water
discloses
its bones

15.

Telesicles, with
these hands that clasp
this jug, we steered
vessels of hardest wood
'cross undulating straits
of grey skin

stretched thin between
the shores of Paros and Thasos;
and we both knew
in tightening sinews

this was no welcome mat
that we were not home.
Though we called it such

and so much depends
on this misdescription
of lands we make
from such friction

16.

Archilochus, what part of us
do we miss most?
I have a host of answers
but no spear.

And neither do I fear
consequence. This
shall end. That follows

and from it
I craft a hollow
from raw earth.

I'll reside there soon enough
granted quick passage
by the curse of your verse.

But as I go, I've one trick to show
modelled on Zeus' trade
of day for night:

you might twitch
with manifold itches,
be owned by myriad pitches

but you'll not
take the hand
of either daughter.

They sail with me.
Then you'll see
to the very bottom
of your body.

I have no gift
to curse, or sing
but bring you much
you must take.

Under it all
your inmost scaffold
must slowly, surely
break

17.

Neobulé, they say
a wolf is keen:
all teeth and stealth
white turned terracotta
at the maw

yet in the hills
and stubbled fields
I only saw
a kindly bite,
the grip at scruff.

The cub a-swing
dangling
above ground

18.

Poseidon, we prayed
receive this craft
Delphi has charged
leave.

We let go
a sea crow
trusting it to chart
the riddling squall

ride aerial paths
above briny brinks
swelling grays and darks
high over moving rocks

questing for that damp
strip of sand beyond
that stripes land

as white horses charge at it
proffering foam
at the mouth

19.

has ever a father
harboured a greater sense
of measure; it hangs
upon him, he

distributes it
across the flesh carriage
he pulls through grass
that blues at dusk

yet is never lost
in the dust cattle disperse
at dawn; nor shaken
in sleep.

A father stores it,
this weight. He is
the deepest pocket,
all jars' distended interiors

20.

I recall
all men aboard
asleep

I recall
the morning snarl
of ibex horn

at sight of shore.
I recall
tension

as knuckle-nests
grip feathered shafts
'gainst polished bow

I recall
the potter's work
knotting and netting shapes

packed in the hold
below deck
to trade

I recall
his fingers exert
wet work

pressing
a hole
in the bowl of a jug

I recall
fingers pull
taut then release

I recall
arrows splash air
slap sand

I recall
other mouths
red at shrieking point

21.

said things
tread close
behind me.

Said things
in flight
as speargrass

barbs all paths,
and clings
to all my loved things.

Said things catch
that tightening patch
of skin

thrumming back
of the drumming ear.
Said things pry

seek out gaps,
dog the tracks
that route trade

to the mutest parts
of a man's acts.
Said things seep

'neath all his doings.
Said things
build his ruins

in struts of straw;
stack tinder
for the flammable whispers

of neighbours,
party leaders,
lawgivers

– hang them all.
Mix the matrix of said things
to a squall.

I am at sea

22.

Amphimedo, it is
as if a confluence of shadows
have fled their kin;

even objects
shed their capes
– nay, spread them

'cross the buttered morning.
I watch them traipse
with neither claim

nor purpose.
They stray. And clay
catches their gait

in the leaving shapes
of worm casts. Or
I swear

these black figures
slip onto pots to be fired
and traded overseas

23.

things that flex,
stretch their shape,
only then to shrink

I think of them;
wings unfurled, then folded
limbs thrust out

then retracted; necks
craned beyond frame,
heads then sunk back.

That moment of expansion,
native to all that moves,
proves its contrary state

of retreat. Telesicles,
Delphi spat us out
had us reach

at gentle stretch, bid us
fetch the unploughed lands
beyond.

Your son sung
of them; lashed all
that crossed him on this path.

The aftermath was spittle,
oft flecked red, leaking
from more than mouth

– and the space
to plant, sew, mine,
mark, cleave and carve

to hand ourselves what's other
in name, knowing
how it came to us

and from whom.

24.

I knew the road god,
Hermes, who trod the path
until it spilt its banks

and there was silt
where none had been;
and I knew then

nothing is clean
or pure. Nor
can our eyes be

adequate to the felting dark

25.

borrow the bile
from a street dog

the stripe
from a wasp

the bite
from the Law

and you will have
no more ingredients

than gods bestow:
we are stirred

yet dammed so
our waters break

climb our sides
as we leak

soft vessels
barely held

26.

there is seasoning
stink under the song

held thick and fast
as a gust at day's middle

or an unnecessary breath
trapped

in the un-expanding chest
of a god

27.

what is it
we cross

joins us
yet divides

clay in the wet
curd beds

taking form
to be traded

in red dawns
on other shores

we send our homes to
dancing

to the forked tongue
of Pythian riddles

28.

Zeus, so
the lizard

leaves its eyelid
behind a film

the cat
puts back its claws

the fox turns
back into its tracks

thus, I retract
my vote

leave it here
on the perimeter

of the agora

29.

Once, approaching Thasos,
night had barely sprung
its trap

whence side-saddled Selene
spilt her silver
over Poseidon's tray

as a slave boy sang
of home
from our prow

the touch of his sounds
circled fields, surrounded tracks
inclined

steep mountain passes
verses feeling
sparse grass

and rock underfoot
lyre netting all
till it slipped

his voice's grip
left his frame
leaving its promise

a labyrinth of holes
tunnelling
his bones

his shape
trembled
snapping like a sail

30.

Amphimedo, you
taught me things
inexplicable to
the body of a god:

how some moving parts
stop, so close to you
whilst all around
continues, persists

filling and falling
spilling and crawling
into other shapes
all this leaving

me
on the edge
joining nothing
save my daughters

31.

of all things
that break
words prove
the deepest splinter

words lead-cold
hold my tongue
a frozen nail

32.

as I hazard the distance
between cup and lip

my grip manages
a slight turn

and the scene changes:
Dolon in black glazed space

paces the undergrowth
on all fours

swallowed
by wolf pelt

and I am ambushed, shipped
slumped ashore

once more on Thasos
in dappled dawn;

we crawl
in crooked steps

as if all the other
were ours

33.

we bore torches
and much else
in the flicker

carried us away
home at our backs
like a shell

we bore torches
and much else
in the flicker

and I know
the thought
of Zeno:

you can remove
the passage of an arrow
but not its point

34.

Old friend undone.
Waves break,
come together,
unharmed.

But a vow
knots tighter
than the absent navel
of a god

and to break it
turns us back
like the fox-fish
flips its skin
inside out
to cough up a hook

35.

a friend sends
sense in words
that shape thought

thicker
than either air's
felting texture

or the flicker
of fire. He grasps
for what mixture makes us

what contrariety
can see us
briefly held.

I turn
to this lunar shield:
moonwort,

it holds its shape
and seeds

36.

Hands.
Do only hands do that,
flex and release?

Un-consuming jaws
that grasp for things
then let fall.

Perhaps only the lungs
model this too.
Amphimedo,

I still feel you
as a promise
tingling at my extremities

when the hours are thinner
than sea skin
at low tide

and dream is
asking me away
– do tell, do answer this riddle:

how do we handle
limbs in sleep, untangle
the arms they flower from?

37.

I put my body
to bed and yet
it will not rest

'cross its parchment breast
are writ in tremor
and twitch

the conquests never made;
they lie beside me
call me

through the medium of touch
such encounters
lease moisture

that breaks in salted dew
for regret
has a body too

your lithe double
liable
to tug at you

38.

of course, fish sleep
beneath, packed
in deep mud pockets

piping bubbles
in the felting dark
whilst I

sat at shore
note the shape
my mouth takes

around a word
it cannot make
out

39.

a father makes
a study of indifference
and the smallest movements

that play the body
in sleep;
that speak

of gifts a god gives
but in whispers
for our ears

won't hear them
are stopped
from doing so

40.

Neobulé, of all the things
I've planted, this
tentative kiss

lands deeper
than the pressure
fingers find

to poke through soil
and hide bulbs

41.

It is now my gift,
thank Zeus,
to produce a catalogue

of things that shrink.
Things wherein
there is a rift

between skin
and what lies
within

42.

poet, master of dyes
your iambic cries
colour us

and we wear
wrong, woven
rudiments of song

43.

the hours shrink, light greys
and I sit like a dish
waiting to be cleared.

The talk
has changed colour
to deepest terracotta.

I hear it bake
in the mouth parts
of the agora

and soon it will break
with over-firing

44.

I angle this jug
and the scene
shimmers

Dolon
under grey pelt
crawls at the night

a spy on all fours
mind a crooked maze
side-stepping

scenting prey
his narrow tongue
primed

to lap
at that
black-watered spring

will belch blood
once the trap
is sprung

– till the tracker
turns tracked:
a wolf dispatched

45.

had we
such a device
could seize

the stuff of seas
plants, and these
remarkable faces

as emotions race them
like grazing clouds
transport shadows across the hills

– still, I'd not will it so;
there's no virtue in holding.
All passes

through

46.

Amphimedo, it is dream
so I wake as dawn decants
on unknown lands

and gently chase
the contours of my face
for signs

your dress has traced
under my sleeping cheek.
I hope to keep them;

may they bake
and fire on these hills
so I might read you

in pattern
and stripe
of softest inscription

47.

sweat frets
my edges

cannot net
my form

yet I go on
to shake it free.

Hermes, gather me
in twine

else I shall break
into brine

48.

kennelled
in the dog days

Sirius governs
with no disguise

under javelin-blue skies

49.

fasten on the sun
with one eye
for you need to squint.

And in that inkling
find the felting world
when it meshes

as if woven; I
am beholden
to notions of opposition.

Give me things
that chafe.
Cherish

the dialogue wave
has with shore
and more:

we flit
as leaves
through the hurtling dark

50.

daughters, did I say
on Thasos

they plough the clay
in great vats

that keep it
capable of shape

qualities the sun
would otherwise take

51.

the rectangle
lodged in the eye
of fox and goat

floats in what?
We have it
held

here
trembles
in the near distance

a wobble
of dirt track
in heat-haze

52.

thorn, scorpion
snake or gall central
to the quilled echidna

your tips are as nothing
to the striped darts
that line my spine

for song
is a lashing tongue
and I leak venom

through the pores of the agora
a standing item
on Dame Harangue's agenda

53.

dust
on the liquid trays
at dusk

just resting
in the halved light,
Zeus.

But on what?
What skin
brings these fine motes

in suspense
peering
under the lip

54.

the skin of a God
glistens not
through exertion

but to mortal eyes
wears the shimmer
of night jewels

or flower-studs
in spring, all voting
for various colours

in exploding meadows.
We bread-eaters are more content,
court animal kin;

I entertain the wryneck
in line, spot and shade
head vacating

its bodily gait;
hail the tortoise shell's
play of pattern

backing the lyre;
or the skin of a snake
like an argumentative sea

bone needles
in woven light
threading the fray

55.

slip
liquid silhouette

join
handle

and jug
trace

spaces
for the kiln

fires us
outlines

so we glaze
black and red figures

.

56.

weights and measures;
scales, poet,
note the eels
in the beet-bed
no longer writhe

but take the red
to their shimmer;
and you partake of it
praying for the long slide
of the crane's throat.

Weights and measures;
scales, poet,
I note your iambic traps
writhe with prey

a slight trickle
wriggles at the creases
of your gloating mouth
as you swallow the day

57.

Amphimedo,
I turn the cup

am halved
by candlelight

years
have yet to pile

your hand
sheathed in mine

we climb mountains on Tenos
and sit in the dust

at dusk.
I am listening

to your inner trickling
so far from any spring

58.

Mother Blame,
Theseus danced geranos
on Delos
with freed slaves

winding

eight steps, leap,
eight steps,
leap

cranes thread
the edges of the world
its ever-turning potter's wheel

winding

eight steps, leap,
eight steps
leap

59.

Poet, I know Apollo
loves you dearly
and sees fit

to not distinguish
between the prongs
of spear, tongue, and song.

I also know
the dappled throat
of a nightingale

wrung at dawn,
sounds day's alarum
as if it rang

inside a helmet
just landed
on a gold-bearing shore

60.

oil and vinegar
poured in the same bowl
only share
when shaken:

Zeus, if it pleases you,
may we stay mixed
and never unfurl

61.

Fox,
you have regaled us.

Your fables
of salt

and overturned tables
fumble at my outlines

I am
neither eagle nor wolf

am spined
like a hedgehog

on Paros
under Sirius

we Lycambids
oath-deep

buried
quarry

62.

wolf steps
across dog days
on blistered pads

watching
the high-climbing goat
keen for the low waters

63.

wants rage
battles in my body
on so many fronts

declare their hot climes
at war for independence
snake the coast path

tongue trade routes
an aftermath
of friction

steps,
steps taken
in the felting dark

I imagine the diction
the trudge of iambs
transporting curses

64.

friend, Telesicles
you know

how the eye
aches

with coming water
like a sky

fit to burst
like friend-fattened seas

65.

Daughters, it is so late
I cannot see. Cannot
think to feel

cannot be he
who builds a canopy
above

when all materials
bring news
of failings

the sapling
too thin
to bare weight

the trap
that falls
from an ass's bony back

the rope
whose fibres fray
like a top knot

slips
across taut shoulders

66.

I sit
in the middle of things
without quarrel
as stars hang in the balance
thread dark between them
some celestial sail cloth
or banner.

In what do we dip
and dye such flags
that it sticks such multiples together
whether they hold common
or not?

I should like
thought to do so
and not sever, slice
or render.

I should have
contraries by my side
sewn into my care
by the love
stitched there.

67.

Bloodless, breathless gods,
all-fasting. I
am asking permission
to tuck ourselves away

as once
you plucked out the sun
over Thasos
and all day we dispensed

with its butter
and all song
vacated bird and beast
alike

68.

Telesicles, what seeds
did we plant by Delphic rote
in the northern climes
of remotest Thasos?

I find no facts
in botanical tracts; no source
to chart the course
of this crop

so thick it grasps all
would harvest it,
sends them home
with a new bloom

that creeps
under the skin
an undisclosed poison.
Friend,

I fear your son
the worm, Lytta
sprouts
under his tongue

69.

each net
its holes

each city
its walls

each body
its exits

each polis
poikilos

founding turbulence
changeling

skin covering snake
and octopus

secreting night
in which to hide

70.

I open my hand
white with the fight
to hold.

The proximity
of father to feather
must never be regulated

71.

I received a word
a barb, a hook,
and mistook its aim

it came for my wits
fried in the breath
of Orion's dog

72.

scheme in beast-speak
poet of fox fur,
though your costume
is muzzle-red

– you'll not dine
on my eaglets:
altar food belongs
to the gods

73.

play dead, fox
of self-cancelling step.
Play rock, octopus; you
sea-knot of all-groping limbs

there are things
cunning cannot trap
though your words prick
the furrows of my back
to a field of waving spear-grass,

stay; see this wolf,
poet, turn hedgehog:
and know my trick
picks your locks

74.

Now, mark
Now, mock
Now, strike
Now, stroke
Now, grip
Now, graze
Now, slip
Now, bend
Now, bid,
Now, blend
Now, build
Now
for
how
else
hold
fast

75.

Murderous Ares,
dice-shaker, you
mover

shake that helmet:

lots

    fall

   prone

76.

when Delphi
dealt her riddling hand
who knew

this wolf
would take the gait
of a lapwing

limping away
from her young.
Come, beast-guides

hosts a-step
ahead
into next lands

77.

let a poet feast
and fatten
fill his word-guts
to their spill

he will not drop
this lardy shield
it clings to him

fox, hedgehog
dog; all bark
and huff, and

leak from their jaws

78.

none shall ever tell
how in young pale light
a father fells a cypress

hacks a mast
that will never sail

79.

look at the sea, poet,
laughing at your words

80.

now
divided

table
turned

salt
spilt

space
laid

Iambe
lodged

wolf
danced

eight steps
– leap

WOLF STEPS: SOME AFTERWORDS

The status of these ancient legends that sketch a crime scene at the birth of lyric remain vexed: we can't know whether Archilochus 'really' used his Iambic prowess to curse Lycambes' family to its grave for a broken marriage oath. But neither can we doubt that his poetic legacy, in Antiquity and beyond, has forced a conjunction between poetry and invective that couldn't be further than notions of purity and elevation that cling to more naïve notions of lyric. His reputation was a by-word for judgements over the acceptability, or otherwise, of indulgence in poetic harm; just as the literary form of Iambic he is famous for is a locus of ethical crises.

The mammoth, in so many ways superlative, anthology of *Lyric Theory*, contains a single reference to Archilochus. And yet my first encounter with this 'first' poet was Fränkel's account of his significance in marking a turn away from impersonal, heroic Epic, to the personal realm of lyric. Key to Fränkel are ideas of softness: the malleable day capable of being shaped by human hands rather than the arbitration of the Gods. He claims, 'Archilochus decisively seizes upon the first and nearest data of the individual: the now, the here, the I' (p. 139). The more I have dug, the deeper I have been immersed in the intricate classical scholarship that has so often contested Fränkel's division – and its implied teleology – between lyric and epic. It has frequently pointed to the more performative elements of Iambic verse as a ceremonial castigation that symbolically plays out ritual events concerning stock characters rather than real individuals. And this final volume explores the central figure pitted in opposition to Archilochus: Lycambes, the father who brings down poetic wrath by calling off the engagement, for reasons history doesn't leave us.

The previous volumes in this Lyric Iambography have dealt with above (exile on the Moon) and below (arrival in Hades). My challenge was where to locate this final part of my Greek trilogy. If Archilochus had the moon, Neobulé Hades, then what stage for Lycambes? The answer was a long time coming, and evasive (as all answers should be). Early on, images of Attic vases and pottery crept into the poems; and it was evident that whereas Archilochus was in exile *after* the havoc he had wrought, and Neobulé arrives in Hades *after* this havoc; Lycambes was inhabiting a multi-faceted present moment *before* he completes his actions by following the death of his daughters with his own. This final volume had to land Lycambes in the less exotic realm of the earth, contemplating his pressing deed, and reminiscing. Central to this reminiscence are his dead wife Amphimedo and the early expeditions to colonise Thasos. He undertook these with Telesicles, Archilochus's father, and that doubtless confirmed, if not established, the bond between the families. My Lycambes undergoes his curse in the Dog Days of summer, whose scorching sun was intricately connected in the Ancient world with the maddening bite of the Iambic bark, and rabies (the Greek term, *Lytta*, was understood as a worm under the tongue of dogs). He clutches the jug that Telesicles bought him in Delphi on the occasion of the visit to the oracle that initiates the mission; a mission that makes Archilochus a soldier poet – many sources suggest a mercenary – and lyric inseparable from colonisation. The images on Lycambes' jug are carefully chosen: on one side a key scene from Book 10 of the *Iliad*, on the other the victory dance of Theseus having freed sacrificial slaves from the Minotaur's labyrinth. Theseus's 'geranos', a Crane dance, is supposed to mimic the winding movement of negotiating the labyrinth and outwitting the maze with the aid of Ariadne's thread. Book 10 of the *Iliad* is devoted to a quality that the Ancients valued highly: stealth. It gives us Dolon (whose name means deceitful cunning) on a spying mission, disguised in grey wolf pelt, to sneak into Odysseus's camp. And yet Odysseus, with higher cunning, ambushes his rival and turns the tables. Detienne and Vernant have written marvellously of Metis, a creative resourcefulness (named after the goddess who eluded Zeus' attentions by constantly shifting shape and size); a specific type of cunning intelligence uniquely equipped to cope with changeable circumstances. For Detienne and Vernant, as they so often are for Archilochus, animals are the focus.

The Slip explores the *ainos* within the surviving fragments, pre-Aesopian fables that were likely stock elements of Iambic verse. The fox is Metis personified, and Aesop's fable of the fox and leopard has the latter's taunt of owning an unmatchable smart coat returned with vulpine wit: 'your coat may be smart, but my wits are smarter still.' The Greek puns further as the word for smart is *poikilos*, a prized ancient concept of perceptual disturbance that celebrates all manner of shimmer and iridescence from the gleam of bronze armour in sunlight to the throat of the Wryneck, and the scales of the snake. The fox's smartness is in having a mottled mind. Archilochus's use of the fable concerning the fox and the eagle is widely regarded as his coded response to being jilted by the Lycambids; and as such, this fragment's animal imagery is the beating heart at the birth of lyric poetry, and yet also the charred remains of the crime scene inseparable from the ancient poet's reputation. In this famous sequence of fragments, the fox recounts his revenge upon the eagle (widely regarded as code for Lycambes) who has betrayed their friendship by eating the vixen's cubs. The fox curses the eagle and appeals to Zeus to intervene and bring justice to bear; the greedy eagle steals meat from a sacrificial altar only to have it burn down his nest and cause its young to fall out into the jaws of its vulpine rival. It is an Archilochean innovation, not present in Aesop, to have the fox pray for Zeus's intervention. In doing so, the poet playfully subverts matters; as Laura Swift has it: 'he draws his audience's attention to the anthropomorphic conventions of fable and takes them to their logical conclusion: a fully anthropomorphised animal would naturally consider that animal-kind was Zeus' special interest and regard men as the bestial "other".'

True to the names of all the 'characters' in Archilochus' biographical tradition, Lycambes is a characternym. His name means 'wolf steps' or 'wolf gait'; and recent scholars have pointed to the 'lupine motif' of the crooked path that creature takes; its deceitful, swerving motion. Deborah Steiner notes the prominence of wolves in the discourse of blame and their strange "locomotory." They are represented in terms of a circling, and this doubling back points to the wolf as figure of a disturbing loss of distinctions, particularly – and most pointedly for the Archilochus legend – that between friend and foe. The hounded Lycambes is also Archilochus's double.

I have borrowed the term 'felting' from Presocratic philosophy, and Anaximenes in particular. He wrote of the primary principle of infinite air 'from which the things that are becoming, and that are, and that shall be, and gods and things divine, all come into being.' He was interested in air's continual motion, and transformation, and used 'felting' to describe air's condensation into other forms (fire, water, even stones).

In pottery, the slip is a liquefied suspension of clay in water and was painted onto the areas of ancient pots intended to emerge black in the firing process. Needless to say, notions of the slip also encompass all manner of acts of evasion, disguise, and the tying of a noose.

So, here are the last steps of the cursed 'wolf walker.'

FURTHER READING
Marcel Detienne, Jean-Pierre Vernant. *Cunning Intelligence in Greek Culture and Society.* 1978
Herman Fränkel, *Early Greek Poetry and Philosophy* trans. Moses Hadas, James Willis. Oxford: Basil Blackell, 1975.
Julia Hawkins, 'The Barking Cure: Horace's "Anatomy of Rage" in Epodes 1, 6, and 16', *American Journal of Philology* 135(1) (March 2014), pp. 57-85
Virginia Jackson, Yopie Prins eds. *The Lyric Theory Reader.* Baltimore, Maryland: Johns Hopkins Press, 2014.
G.S. Kirk, J.E. Raven eds. *The Presocratic Philosophers.* Cambridge: Cambridge University Press, 1957.
Deborah Steiner, 'Wolf's Justice': The Iliadic Doloneia and the semiotics of Wolves. *Classical Antiquity*, vo.34, no.2 (Oct 2015), pp335-369
Laura Swift, 'The animal fable and Greek iambus: ainoi and half-ainoi in Archilochus' In C. Werner and B. Sebastini (edd.) *Gêneros poéticos na Grécia antiga: Confluências e fronteiras, Humanitas,* 2014: 49-77.